Jo Sherry

D0390572

WHEN YOUR PET DIES

Love Val

Also by Alan Wolfelt

Healing Your Grieving Heart
100 Practical Ideas

Healing a Child's Grieving Heart
100 Practical Ideas for Families, Friends and Caregivers

Healing a Teen's Grieving Heart
100 Practical Ideas for Families, Friends and Caregivers

Healing Your Grieving Heart for Kids
100 Practical Ideas

Healing Your Grieving Heart for Teens
100 Practical Ideas

The Journey Through Grief
Reflections on Healing

Understanding Your Grief
Ten Essential Touchstones for Finding Hope and Healing Your Heart

The Understanding Your Grief Journal
Exploring the Ten Essential Touchstones

Companion
P R E S S

Companion Press is dedicated to the education and support
of both the bereaved and bereavement caregivers.

We believe that those who companion the bereaved by
walking with them as they journey in grief have a wondrous
opportunity: to help others embrace and grow through
grief–and to lead fuller, more deeply-lived lives
themselves because of this important ministry.

For a complete catalog and ordering information,
visit our website, write, or call:

Companion Press
The Center for Loss and Life Transition
3735 Broken Bow Road
Fort Collins, CO 80526
(970) 226-6050
www.centerforloss.com

WHEN YOUR PET DIES

A GUIDE TO MOURNING, REMEMBERING, AND HEALING

Alan D. Wolfelt, Ph.D.

Companion
PRESS

Fort Collins, Colorado
An imprint of the Center for Loss and Life Transition

Companion Press is an imprint of the Center for Loss and Life Transition, 3735 Broken Bow Road, Fort Collins, Colorado 80526
www.centerforloss.com

Companion Press books may be purchased in bulk for sales promotions, premiums or fundraisers. Please contact the publisher at the above address for more information.

Printed in the United States of America

13 12 11 10   5 4 3 2

ISBN: 978-1-879651-36-4

In memory of Tasha and Keesha

CONTENTS

INTRODUCTION   1

PART ONE: MOURNING   3

PART TWO: REMEMBERING   37

PART THREE: HEALING   53

A FINAL WORD   73

THE PET LOVER'S CODE   77

RESOURCES   79

Love all God's creation, the whole of it and every grain of sand. Love every leaf, every ray of God's light; love the beasts, love the plants, love every creature. If you love everything, you will perceive the divine mystery in things. And once you have perceived it, you will begin to comprehend it ceaselessly, more, more, and more every day. And you will come at last to love the whole world with an abiding universal love. Love the animals: God has given them the rudiments of thought and untroubled joy.

Fyodor Dostoevsky

Here's a photograph of my special pet that died:

Name of my pet_____

Year of birth_____ - Year of death_____

INTRODUCTION

In my boyhood I loved a Toy Manchester named Chico. He was an affectionate dog that slept with me every night and had a habit of resting his black and brown head on my leg, ears cocked, letting me know he was ready and waiting to play whenever I was. When I was 12, he darted out our back door and was immediately struck and killed by a car.

I was devastated. I was angry. I was sad. I was bereaved. Chico's death was my first introduction to loss, and what a hard introduction it seemed to me at the time.

In the years since then, I have been the loving owner of a German Shepherd and a succession of Siberian Huskies. At this writing I have three Huskies–Lexi, Dani, and Nikki. All are a part of my heart and my family. I call them "my furriest children."

I grew up to be a grief counselor and educator. It has been a true privilege to "walk with" and learn from thousands of mourners. I have traveled North America extensively, teaching–and being taught–about grief and mourning. I have counseled many mourners at my Center for Loss and Life Transition here in the foothills west of Fort Collins, Colorado.

Many of these people have shared with me the impact that the death of a pet has had on their lives, indeed, their very beings. You will find a number of these "real life" stories, in the mourner's own words, sprinkled throughout this book. But to truly empathize with these stories, I don't need to call upon all my years of formal education. I only need to open the heart of that 12-year-old boy I was and recall my profound feelings of grief and loss.

This book is for people who grieve after the death of a special pet and who need help mourning, remembering, and healing. Whether you are a dog lover, as I am, or your special pet was a cat, a horse, a bird, a goat, or any other companion animal you loved and cared for, my hope is that this book is a supportive companion to you. After all, what matters is not the kind of animal you love but the love you have for the animal!

This book was written to help you understand why your grief can feel so hurtful and how you can mourn your feelings of grief to help integrate them into your life. It will also give you ideas and a safe place for remembering your pet, so that years from now you will always have a record of your special companion animal. Finally, this book will help you heal, for it is through mourning and remembering that we heal after any death.

I invite you to engage with this book with an open mind and an open heart. Be honest, brave and true–just as your pet was, so you must be now. Let us begin.

PART ONE
MOURNING

Your beloved companion animal has died. I am so very sorry for your loss.

Your grief is a journey that started on the day that your special pet died. Actually, if your pet was sick or in declining health before she died, your grief was set in motion when you first understood that the illness would result in death.

An important distinction to keep in mind as you read this book is the difference between grief and mourning. Grief is the constellation of internal thoughts and feelings we have when someone we love dies. In other words, grief is the internal meaning given to the experience of loss. Mourning is when you take the grief you have on the inside and express it outside of yourself. Mourning is the outward expression of grief.

In Part One of this book, you will learn not only about common thoughts and feelings of grief after the death of a pet, but ways to mourn those thoughts and feelings, as well. Over time and with the support of others, to mourn is to heal.

The capacity to love requires the necessity to mourn

When a pet dies, you may feel the loss very strongly. You may feel overwhelmed by the depth of your sadness. Others, especially those who have never experienced the joy of giving and receiving love from a pet, may not understand your feelings of loss. They may even imply that you are overreacting.

If you take away only one piece of counsel from this book, let it be this: Your feelings are what they are. The fact that you are having these feelings means you need to have them. Never shame yourself over feelings of love and loss.

The second piece of counsel I hope you take from this book is that you need to express your feelings. The outward expression of grief, or mourning, is how you externalize those thoughts and feelings and ultimately, integrate them into your life.

If your grief feels very painful and debilitating, your brain might be asking your heart why this is so. Following are a few of the main reasons that our beloved companion animals are so important to us.

AN HISTORICAL PERSPECTIVE

The strong bond between people and animals is not a recent phenomenon. Actually, it dates all the way back to ancient times. Archeologists have discovered prehistoric gravesites that prove that people were often buried with their dogs. The early Egyptians thought so much of their cats that when a beloved cat died, the owners shaved off their own eyebrows to acknowledge the loss. This was a way to let others know they were in mourning and needed support. So, as you mourn your pet, remember—people have always loved their pets and mourned their deaths.

Pets are part of our families

Most pet owners I know consider their pets part of their families. A recent survey showed that at least a third of dog owners consider their dogs to be family members. I'd guess that the actual number is much higher.

How do our pets come to be considered a part of our families? Well, we not only love our family members, but we're concerned about their well-being. We make sure they receive good medical care and eat good food. We encourage them to get exercise. We give them comfortable places to sleep. Sound like your pet so far?

With family members, we also enjoy their presence in our everyday lives. We come home glad to see them and they to see us. We look forward to spending time with each other. When we're with them, no matter where we are, we're "home."

Of course our beloved pets are part of our families.

Pets delight in our company

We pet lovers sometimes call our pets "companion animals" because they are, in fact, our companions. In fact, the majority of dog owners (68%) and cat owners (61%) say that companionship is the main reason they have a pet. You could even say that our pets' very purpose is to spend time with us and simply "be" with us.

Not only are our pets our companions, but they also help meet our need for physical contact. How many companions in our lives do we routinely hug and hold and kiss? Compared to the physical intimacy we experience with a partner and the physical closeness we might share with our children, our use of touch with our pets is often as or more frequent. We touch our pets and they seek out our touch. We are comforted, calmed, and grounded when we stroke them or they lie next to us. When death separates us from our pets physically, we mourn not only the loss of a companion, but a companion whose touch was central to the relationship.

HOW MUCH DO WE LOVE OUR PETS?

- 95% of dog owners hug their dogs daily
- 85% of cat owners play with their cats daily
- 45% have taken their dogs on vacation
- 29% have celebrated their cat's birthday

While I was unable to find similar statistics for horse owners, bird owners, etc., I'm sure they would be equally telling of our love for all our companion animals.

Pets are part of the ritual of our days

Because pets are part of our families, they are an important part of the ritual of our days. If your special pet was an indoor animal, you may have awoken with the pet near you and expressing his affection for you each morning. All pets require nourishment; you may have begun your day by feeding your pet—perhaps before you fed others in your family or even yourself! (My pets get fed before I even make my coffee in the morning.)

Grooming and exercising your pet may also have been a regular part of your routine. And it is likely that your pet's presence played other, subtler (but just as important) parts in your day. Maybe your dog

A horse called Starlight Moon
Kirby's story

She had a white star on her forehead, a pretty sorrel color to her coat, and because she was born under a full moon, I named her Starlight Moon. Since my childhood on a Wyoming ranch I had always wanted to raise a foal of my own and as an adult I finally got the chance with Starlight.

One day, Starlight hurt her leg. I took her to the veterinary hospital and after spending several thousand dollars on tests, X-rays and nerve conduction studies, I found out she had a radial nerve palsy with at least a possibility of recovery. Even if she could never be a sound horse, maybe she could be a broodmare, I reasoned. Twice daily for months I removed her splint, performed physical therapy on her leg and redressed her leg. It was very time-consuming, but she whinnied at me each time I came and seemed to appreciate the time we spent together. She was always cooperative, even when the therapy was not pleasant. Eventually I was able to wean her to smaller and smaller splints until she was able to stand and walk without too much of a limp.

Just as I was beginning to feel optimistic, one morning I noticed her standing stiffly, unwilling to move at all. She was now lame on all her legs. Once again the vet returned with woeful news. She had foundered from the stress of the injury; the bones in her feet had become inflamed and her hooves had grown irregularly. She was now in constant pain. This time I agreed to let the vet put her down.

It was quick and painless, but I still remember the sound as she fell to the ground from the injection. I moved her in a trailer to the corner of the pasture, where I had dug a grave. After I buried her, we had a ceremony at the gravesite in which my wife, our three kids, and I all recalled our favorite moments with Starlight. At the end I said a short prayer and left her spirit in the hands of God. I planted a rose on the gravesite. Sometimes I still look for her in the pasture. And occasionally I see her running through the green grass in my mind.

always sat at your feet while you read the newspaper. Perhaps your horse greeted you with a fond whinny when you walked out to get the mail each day. Maybe you spent some time in affectionate play with your pet every evening.

In many ways, pets are an intrinsic part of our day-to-day lives. Their absence, then, comes as a shock. Not only has a companion you dearly loved been taken from you, but a key piece of the ritual of your life suddenly is no longer. No wonder it can feel like your life has been torn apart.

IT'S ALL IN A DAY'S WORK—FOR A PET

Have you noticed that more and more companies are encouraging employees to bring their pets to work? A recent study by the American Pet Products Manufacturers Association found that having a pet in the office results in better motivation, more productivity and decreased absenteeism. In addition, many health-enhancing benefits of pet ownership, from reduced blood pressure to lower stress levels to improved overall health, carry over into the office environment. This trend is testament to the depth of the relationships we have with our pets—and the depth of the loss when they die.

Pets give us unconditional love

A final reason that our pets are so very important to us is that they give us that rarest of affirmations–unconditional love.

Our pets love us no matter how lazy we are, how slovenly, how unsuccessful. They don't expect great things of us; they don't pressure us to work harder or earn more money. Our pets love us regardless of our weight or haircut or body shape.

Our pets love us without judgment. They even love us when we don't love them back as well as we should—when we neglect to groom them or take them to the vet or forget their night-time meal.

They love us. They just do. And we feel that love and appreciate its steadfast presence in our lives.

Grieving a pet vs. grieving a person: Is it the same thing?

In my travels throughout North America teaching about grief and loss, I'm often tacitly asked to acknowledge that some types of loss are more difficult than others. Yes, the death of a child is an excruciating experience for parents. The death of a spouse can also be very hard for the widow left behind. Deaths by homicide and suicide often result in extremely painful and complicated grief for mourners. But none of these kinds of death is definitively the "worst" for family and friends. You simply cannot "rank" losses in this objective, overarching way, because each particular death, no matter the cause or circumstances, is colored by infinite variables.

And what of the death of a pet? Isn't a pet less important than a person? And so shouldn't we feel less grief after the death of a pet?

Here's what I know to be true: Pet owners often feel the loss of their companion animals very deeply. If asked to explain the significance of the loss, many will say it was one of the most profound in their lives because (and here' s the important part) the relationship they had with their pet was one of the most profound in their lives.

9

Wally the parrot
Jean's story

My husband and I would both attest that our attachment to Wally, a Senegal parrot, was the most intense attachment either of us has ever had to an animal (and we have both had dogs, cats, hamsters, etc.). Birds are intimate companions; they crave physical contact with you, engage in continuous verbal interplay with you, want to be in the same room with you, and bond strongly to you. And parrots even express their wishes; they talk to you. So when you have a parrot, you don't have a pet. You develop a relationship. And I would say that my relationship to Wally was one of the most significant relationships I've had in my life, animal or human.

One day I was lying on my bed reading; Wally was on a T-stand looking out the window. He sneezed a few times and then called me to him. I went to him and as he stepped onto my hand, he keeled over backwards. (And because parrots have a reflex that causes their digits to grasp when they lean back, instead of falling to the ground, he was hanging from my finger). I tried to resuscitate him for much longer than was logical, then called my husband at work and gave into hysteria. Chris rushed home and I wouldn't stop cradling this dead little parrot body, sobbing. I had a small, unreasonable hope that he would somehow come back to life if I held him long enough.

This summer it will be eight years since Wally died. He's still very much present in the secret language Chris and I have that consists of Wally's phrases and voice; in the pretty glass vase that holds his molted feathers; and in all the damaged household items: clothing with holes, expensive pens with bite marks, frayed furniture, file folders with chewed edges, books partially shredded—beak destruction that made us furious when it happened, but now makes things special. But Wally is most present, I think, in the way that Chris and I have never had another pet. I think in a way we're afraid to put that much love into a pet again, or afraid that we couldn't love another as much.

People are often closer to their pets than they are to other human beings. We spend time with our pets day in and day out, whereas we might see our family infrequently. And our relationships with our pets are often less complicated than our relationships with other people. They are more straightforward and consistently happy, whereas our relationships with other people are often complicated and ambivalent.

I believe that grief for a pet is not inferior to or "less than" any other grief. It is what it is. If you feel it deeply and profoundly, then the loss is deep and profound for you and, as with any grief, is a result of the deep and profound love you felt for the pet that died. Only you can be the judge of your grief after your pet dies. Accept it for what it is and mourn it accordingly.

How your grief is unique

Everyone grieves after the death of a beloved companion animal. But their grief is never precisely the same as anyone else's. Each person's grief is shaped by all the things that make each of us unique human beings.

Your grief over the death of your pet will be affected by:

- **The nature of the relationship you had with your pet.**
  As I've already said, the stronger the attachment, the deeper the grief. Some people are even dependent upon their pets for their own survival! When a guide dog dies, the implications for his blind master can be profound. The length of the relationship you had with your pet will also be a factor. And some human-pet relationships are ambivalent. When my Huskies are puppies and chewing on my furniture, I often say I have a love-hate relationship with

WHEN AN OLDER ADULT'S PET DIES

For older adults, their relationships with their pets are often the most meaningful relationships they have in their present lives. Under these circumstances, the pet becomes a "very best friend." And so the pet's death can have a significant impact, particularly if the older adult is isolated from human contact.

My 76-year-old mother lives in an assisted living facility with her little rat terrier, Minnie. "She's a lot of company," Mom says. "I don't know what I'd do without her."

When the pet dies, the experience may trigger old griefs from losses encountered throughout life. It may also cause the elderly person to lose all hope for the future and despair the lonely weeks and years to come. On the other hand, many older people, having coped with death many times before, reconcile themselves to the loss of their pets with relative ease.

Older adults may need to talk about their grief over the death of a pet, sometimes telling the same stories over and over again. Finding one or two good listeners who will listen without judgment can make all the difference.

They also need encouragement to mourn in other ways, such as journaling or painting or planting a garden in memory of their pet. These activities help direct their time and focus and give meaningful shape to the early days and weeks of intense grief.

Also, don't inappropriately push a new pet on an older adult. Knowing that a new pet might outlive them, some make the selfless, responsible decision not to get another pet. Choosing to remain petless is not necessarily a sign of complicated grief or withdrawal.

them! Having mixed feelings about a pet when she is alive can lead to mixed feelings upon her death.

• The circumstances of the death.

Sometimes how and why your pet died will play a big part in your grief. If your pet was ill for a long time and had to endure pain, you may be troubled by this aspect of the loss. If your pet's death was sudden or violent (such as being hit by a car), you will probably need to spend more time processing the circumstances of the death before you can truly mourn the loss of the life.

• Your unique personality.

Whatever your unique personality, it will be reflected in your grief. For example, if you tend to be quiet and introverted, you may express your grief quietly. If you are outgoing, you may be more expressive of your grief.

• Your support systems.

The quality and the quantity of support you feel from people around you as you mourn the death of your pet has a decided impact on your grief. If you have caring, nonjudgmental people to talk to about your loss, people who will really listen and respond with empathy, your journey to healing will be easier. If you don't have family, friends, or co-workers to talk to about your loss, consider joining a pet loss support group.

• Other crises or stresses in your life right now.

What else is going on in your life right now? Although we often wish it wouldn't, the world does keep turning when we are in grief. And whatever your specific situation, I'm sure that your grief is not the only stress in your life right now. The more intense and numerous the stresses in your life, the more overwhelming your grief experience may be. Or, sometimes your grief will be naturally delayed because of the other stresses you are faced with.

What else is shaping your unique grief journey? There are probably other factors, large and small, that are influencing your grief over the death of your special companion animal right now. What are they? I invite you to think about them and write about them here:

_____

_____

_____

_____

_____

_____

_____

_____

_____

_____

_____

_____

_____

_____

_____

_____

_____

_____

_____

_____

_____

Katie the dog
Chris's story

Katie was an Australian Shepherd/Border Collie mix that Gary and I got at the Humane Society before we had our daughter. She was part of our young married life, going for runs with Gary and hikes with me. We were very close to her, but then when Jana was born, my loyalties shifted to Jana, and I'm ashamed to say I think I took out some of my frustrations on Katie—never physically, but sometimes getting mad in her presence and not being as physically loving as I was with her before.

Anyway, we all lived happily together after Jana left the baby stage, and Katie was a big part of Jana's life. She was 14 the year that Jana was eight, and we knew she would die soon; she had hip dysplasia, and sometimes couldn't climb steps, or lift her back end very well. Then, the summer of 1992, Jana and I went to Vermont to visit my sister. While we were gone, Katie got sick and had to be put down. Poor Gary—he had to handle it by himself.

Anyway, we got home, and for Jana and I it was surreal. Katie wasn't there, but we hadn't seen her die, and I think we really missed out. Gary said he wished we'd been there so we could all have cried together, and I think we missed out in that experience as a family, too.

So now she was gone. I had "made up" with her two years earlier, and apologized to her for not being nice those years when Jana was little. I remember the day I did it. I went to pet her, and her whole body shuddered in relief, like she knew I had "come back" to her emotionally. And although I had complained about having to walk her every day because I couldn't go where I wanted or as fast as I wanted, after she died, I didn't want to walk at all. It was too lonely. And too empty.

A year later we went to the Humane Society and got a dog that looked exactly like Katie. In fact, we wondered if it WAS Katie reincarnated. Her name is Jasmine. Now I don't remember Katie very well, but I love Jasmine with a passion. Is that good or right? I like to think that Katie is a part of Jasmine.

What you may be feeling

You may be feeling many strong and strange feelings since the death of your pet. Rather than deny your feelings, I want to help you learn to recognize and learn from them.

My goal here is to help you see how normal your grief thoughts, feelings and behaviors are after the death of a pet. I have worked with many pet lovers after a special pet has died and they have taught me about many different thoughts and feeling. Rest assured that whatever you are thinking and feeling, while in one sense your thoughts and feelings are completely unique to you, they are also usually a common human response to loss. And keep in mind that even if you haven't experienced some of these thoughts and feelings so far, you may do so in the future.

COMMON FEELINGS AFTER THE DEATH
OF A SPECIAL PET

- shock and disbelief
- disorganization and confusion
- physical symptoms
- explosive emotions
- sadness and depression
- relief and release

Shock and disbelief

When your pet dies, your first response may be one of shock and disbelief. "This feels like a dream," you might think. "This can't be happening." In the early hours and days, you may feel numb and, like

16

your mouth after it has been numbed at the dentist's office, unable to truly feel the full impact of the loss.

Thank goodness for shock and disbelief! These feelings are nature's way of temporarily protecting you from the full reality of a death. On one level, you know your pet is dead. But on other, deeper levels, you are not yet able or willing to truly believe it. This mixture of shock, numbness and disbelief acts as an anesthetic: The pain exists, but you may not experience it fully.

Disorganization and confusion

After the death of your beloved pet, you may feel disorganized and distracted. You may feel unable to complete tasks. You may start to do something but never finish. You may feel forgetful and ineffective, and may experience fatigue throughout the day. This is so common it is called "the lethargy of grief." Everyday pleasures may not seem to matter anymore.

You also may experience a restless searching for the pet that has died. Yearning and preoccupation with memories can leave you feeling drained. You may spend large parts of your day remembering times you shared with your pet and wishing that he or she could return to you.

You may also dream about the pet that died. Dreams can be an unconscious means of searching for a pet that is gone. Be careful not to over-interpret your dreams. Simply remain open to learning from them. If the dreams are pleasant, embrace them; if they are disturbing, find someone who'll understand to talk to about them.

Other common experiences during this time include difficulties eating and sleeping. You may experience a loss of appetite, or find yourself overeating. Even when you do eat, you may be unable to taste the food. Having trouble falling asleep and early morning awakening are also common experiences associated with this dimension of grief.

Physical symptoms

Your body may be letting you know it feels distressed. Actually, one literal definition of the word "grievous" is "causing physical suffering." You may be shocked by how much your body responds to the impact of the loss.

Muscle aches and pains, shortness of breath, feelings of emptiness in your stomach, tightness in your throat or chest, digestive problems, sensitivity to noise, heart palpitations, queasiness, nausea, headaches, increased allergic reactions, changes in appetite, weight loss or gain, agitation, and generalized tension--these are all ways your body may react to the death of a special pet.

Among the most common physical responses to loss are troubles with sleeping and low energy. You may have difficulty getting to sleep. Perhaps even more commonly, you may wake up early in the morning and have trouble getting back to sleep. During your grief journey, your body needs more rest than usual. You may also find yourself getting tired more quickly.

Right now you may not feel in control of how your body is responding. Your body is communicating with you about the stress you are experiencing! Keep in mind, however, that in the majority of instances, the physical symptoms described above are normal and temporary. If you have any physical symptoms that are worrying you, by all means see a physician for a check-up. Sometimes ruling out underlying illness will help you feel more at ease.

Freddie the horse
Anne's story

I got my horse Freddie when I was 10. His owner was moving to Arizona and thought that at 24, Freddie was too old to withstand the trip and the heat. When the owner left, he was happy to have found Freddie a good home and gave me an angel ornament. At that time I was homeschooled and spent every afternoon riding Freddie near my house. He was a great horse and we became good friends over the years. In 2001 Freddie was in his early 30s and got a very bad case of colic. The vet could do nothing for him so we had to have him put down.

I knew it was for the best and that he had lived a long life, but his death was still very hard for me. Freddie and I had spent a lot of time together and many days discovering new things on our rides. When he died it was like losing a best friend. I had always given Freddie a peppermint on Christmas morning, so the Christmas after his death I put a peppermint on his grave. The ornament the previous owner had given me is also very special and even if I put nothing else on the holiday tree, I always hang up "Freddie's angel."

Explosive emotions

Anger, hate, blame, resentment, and rage are explosive emotions that may be a volatile yet natural part of your grief journey after the death of a cherished companion animal. It helps to understand that all these feelings are, at bottom, a form of protest. Think of the toddler whose favorite toy is yanked out of his hands. This toddler wants the toy; when it's taken, his instinctive reaction may be to scream or cry or hit. When a beloved pet is taken from you, your instinctive reaction may be much the same.

I was furious when my dog Chico was killed. I was mad at the family member who left the door open for him to run out of. I was angry at the driver of the car that killed him. I was even mad at the neighbor boy who came over to my house the next day and nonchalantly said, "I heard your dog got killed." Really, I felt helpless, but it expressed itself as protest, and this helped me survive.

If your pet died as a result of an accident, you may feel mad, too. You might blame those whom you feel are at fault, even if in your mind you know the death was truly an accident. If your pet died after an illness, you may feel anger and resentment at the veterinary staff— even though you may rationally know they did everything they could.

Unfortunately, our society doesn't understand how normal and necessary these feelings can be. The implicit message is that you should try to "keep it together"—especially since this is "only" about the death of a pet! When you're openly angry, others may get upset. The intensity of your own emotions may even upset you. Still, you must give yourself permission to feel whatever you feel and to express those feelings. Do remember—these feelings will soften over time as you allow yourself to openly mourn.

Lucyfish
Olivia's story

One day my daughter's fish, named Lucyfish after her favorite cousin, just stopped swimming. Olivia was so sad when we found that Lucyfish wasn't breathing anymore. At first Olivia thought she was just playing the "freeze" game or sleeping when we found her floating at the top of the water. When we talked about her dying, Olivia cried. She asked lots of tough questions that she thought Mommy could answer. "Why did she die?" "Will she be alive again Mommy?" "If we get another fish, will she die too?" Over the next few hours we talked many times, usually for just a few minutes, about Lucyfish. We decided that it would help if we found a way to say goodbye.

There were only two of us there, but Olivia and myself shared an experience that I know neither of us will forget. Olivia wanted to play a "water song," so she picked out a song called the Wonders of the Ocean from a Nature Sounds disc. We lit a scented white candle that sat on the back of the potty while we said our goodbyes to Lucyfish. While I held Lucyfish, Olivia told her how much she loved her and wouldn't forget her. She told her that she would miss feeding her and watching her swim. Olivia and I both blew Lucyfish a kiss. We put her gently in the water together, and closed the lid. Olivia told Lucyfish she would never forget her, and almost a year later, she still talks about this little red fish who was loved more than she will ever know.

Olivia also wanted to share her story about Lucyfish in her own words:

Lucyfish was a fish. She ate fish food. Everyday she would swim, swim, swim. And I really miss her 'cause she died. I really, really love her. I love her because she was my fish. She was red and she was a girl and she liked flowers, like me. I had her for a little bit but I love her a lot, lot, lot. Lucyfish I miss you and I love you.
Olivia, 4½ years old

21

WHEN A CHILD'S PET DIES

The death of a pet is often a child's first introduction to death. And for children, as for us, the death of a beloved pet is a significant loss. As caring adults, we have the opportunity and responsibility to respond in ways that empower children to mourn their pets. Your response during this time can determine whether your children's experience will be a positive or negative part of their personal growth and development.

• Model your own feelings about the death of the pet. If you do so, children will have a model for expressing their own feelings.

• But do not coerce children into mourning in the same way you do. Children, while very capable of mourning, often project a "short sadness span" and can go from sadness to joyful play and back again frequently, with the sadness overtaking them in very brief spurts. This is normal and natural.

• When appropriate, explain that the pet's illness and death was no one's fault. Some children feel they are responsible because they forgot to feed the dog or pay attention to the cat.

• Use simple and direct language in sharing facts about the death. Do not make up stories or tell half-truths to protect children.

• If euthanasia is used, do not describe it as "putting the pet to sleep." Children need to understand that sleep and death are not the same thing. Instead, explain euthanasia as a quick, painless way to help a suffering pet die.

- Encourage involvement in ritual. Children use the funeral ceremony of a pet to help them understand the death and mourn the loss.

- Encourage creative outlets for feelings—writing a poem or a story about the pet, creating a memory book or planting a tree in the pet's memory are just a few of many ways to help children mourn the pet's death.

- Openly discuss what will be done with the pet's body. This helps children feel involved and they can often participate in the process.

- Do not attempt to replace the dead pet before the child has an opportunity to mourn. After time, it may be appropriate to suggest finding another pet—not to take to take the place of the previous pet but to enter the family as a new member.

A kitten's accidental death
John's story

About a year ago, we had a five-month-old kitten that died by the name of Kitty Boo. The kitten belonged to my daughter, Bailee, 4, and son, Joshua, 2. He was a very affectionate cat and loved lying on my children's laps. They were extremely attached to him.

One Saturday, the cat had gotten out of the house and into the garage without my wife's knowledge. My wife and kids got in the car to run an errand and accidentally backed over Kitty Boo. My wife called me at work hysterical that she had killed the kitten. Needless to say, I rushed home to find my wife in the car still with the kids. The kids were crying, as was my wife.

We took the kids inside to draw pictures for Kitty Boo and I got a shoe box and placed the cat inside with the towel. We invited my in-laws to come over and we all had a little service out back and said our good-byes. My kids put their pictures in with Kitty Boo and we tied the box shut with a ribbon and some flowers.

We then proceeded to the 'cemetery' (in the back corner of our yard), where we buried Kitty Boo and said our final goodbyes. Within a few minutes, my kids were back to normal and running around the yard, although they did have a few questions off and on, especially my daughter, for a few days afterward.

We ordered a bronze kitty marker on a granite base with the name Kitty Boo and the dates. We placed the marker in the flower garden on his grave. Several months later, my daughter had a friend over to play and she said, 'Do you want to see my cat?' The friend replied, 'Sure' and they began to run toward the corner of the yard. As they approached the grave, my daughter said, 'He's dead' and showed her the grave. After a few moments of looking at the marker and talking, they were off again. This has since happened a few other times.

I would say my kids still consider Kitty Boo a part of the family and now and then they say they "miss Kitty Boo."

Guilt and regret

Guilt, regret and self-blame are common and natural feelings after a death. You may have a case of the "if-onlys": If only I had gotten him to the vet sooner... If only I hadn't let him out the side gate... If only I had been more responsible...

If you find yourself experiencing these if-onlys, be compassionate with yourself. There are limits to your responsibility for this pet. You loved him and took care of him as best you could. He appreciated your love and care.

While these feelings of guilt and regret are natural, they are sometimes not logical to those around you. When you express your guilt and regret, some people may say, "Don't be silly. There was nothing you could have done." Whether you could have done something or not is beside the point. The point is that you are feeling like you could have or should have and you need to express those feelings, however illogical. The important thing to remember is to find understanding people who will bear witness to your multitude of thoughts and feelings.

Sadness and depression

Sadness can be the most hurtful feeling on your journey through grief after the death of a pet. We don't want to be sad. Sadness saps pleasure from our lives. Sadness makes us feel crummy. As Americans, our Constitution even says we have a right to life, liberty and "the pursuit of happiness."

But sadness is a natural, authentic emotion after a death. Something precious in your life is now gone. Of course you are sad. Of course you feel deep sorrow. Allowing yourself to feel your sadness is in large part what your journey toward healing is all about. I suggest you say out loud right now, "I have every right to feel sad!"

Unfortunately, our culture has an unwritten rule that says while physical illness is usually beyond our control, emotional distress is your fault. In other words, some people think you should be able to "control" or subdue your feelings of sadness. Nothing could be further from the truth. Your sadness is a symptom of your wound. Just as physical wounds require attention, so do emotional and spiritual wounds.

Paradoxically, the only way to lessen your pain is to move toward it, not away from it. Moving toward your sadness is not easy to do. Every time you admit to feeling sad, people around you may say things like, "Oh, don't be sad" or "Get a hold of yourself" or "Just think about what you have to be thankful for." Comments like these hinder, not help, your healing. If your heart and soul are prevented from feeling the sadness, odds are your body may be harmed in the process. You have been emotionally, physically and spiritually injured. Now you must attend to your injury.

Normal grief vs. clinical depression

In many ways, depression and grief are similar. Common shared symptoms are feelings of sadness, lack of interest in usually pleasurable activities, and problems with eating and sleeping. The central difference is that while grief is a normal, natural, and healthy process, clinical depression is not.

Normal Grief	Clinical Depression
You have normal grief if you...	You may be clinically depressed if you...
__ respond to comfort and support.	__ do not accept support.
__ are often openly angry.	__ are irritable and complain but do not directly express anger.
__ relate your depressed feelings to the loss experience.	__ do not relate your feelings of depression to a particular life event.
__ can still experience moments of enjoyment in life.	__ exhibit an all-pervading sense of doom.
__ exhibit feelings of sadness and emptiness.	__ project a sense of hopelessness and chronic emptiness.
__ may have transient physical complaints.	__ have chronic physical complaints.
__ express guilt over some specific aspect of the loss.	__ have generalized feelings of guilt.
__ feel a temporary loss of self-esteem.	__ feel a deep and ongoing loss of self-esteem.

If you suspect you are clinically depressed, it is critically important that you take steps to get help. Untreated depression can raise your risk for a number of additional health problems. It also may prevent you from moving forward in your journey through grief. You deserve to get help so you can continue to mourn in ways that help you heal.

Relief and release

Sometimes you may feel a sense of relief and release when a pet dies. The death may have brought relief from suffering, particularly following an illness that was long and perhaps painful. Your relief, then, is normal and natural. Understand that your relief, however, does not equate to a lack of love for the pet that died. In fact, it is often an expression of the depth of your love.

Another form of relief you may experience comes when you finally express your thoughts and feelings about the death of your beloved pet. If you have repressed or denied these feelings before, when you do express them you may feel as if a great pressure has been lifted from your head, heart, and soul.

If you've chosen euthanasia

Choosing to euthanize a pet is a heartrending decision. If you have chosen to euthanize your pet, the most important thing you can do is to trust and accept that you made the right choice.

The word euthanasia comes to us from the Greek word that means "happy or fortunate in death." Together you and your veterinarian decided that what was best for your beloved companion animal was a swift and sure end to his suffering. You wanted him to be "happy in death."

I hope you were able to spend some private time with your pet before and maybe during the procedure. Your presence calmed your pet and let him know that he was being cared for and loved.

Still, even though you made the right choice for you and your pet, you should keep in mind that your grief will be affected by the

MISCONCEPTIONS ABOUT PET GRIEF

Our society fosters a number of misconceptions about the pet lover's grief after the death of a pet. Don't allow yourself to buy into these misconceptions; if you do, you will feel ashamed of your grief and your healing will be hindered.

You don't need to grieve because it was just a pet.
If you give love and receive love in return, you are in a relationship. If that relationship is severed by death, you will grieve. This is normal and natural.

It hurts less because it was just a pet.
How much it hurts in death is a product of how much love and attachment there was in life. This is true in human relationships as well as in human-animal relationships. If you deeply loved your pet and felt a strong bond with him, you will probably hurt deeply.

If you cry too much after a pet dies, you're being too emotional.
When we're in grief, crying helps us express that grief. So crying is a form of mourning. Crying is also nature's way of releasing internal tensions in the body. If people around you are uncomfortable with your tears, find others who can be comfortable with your tears or retreat to somewhere private when it's time to have a good cry.

Pets don't have souls so they can't go to heaven.
Now I'm not a theologian, and I know that various organized religions weigh in differently on this matter, but as a pet lover I can tell you that my dogs had souls and I expect to see them again one day. When it comes to this matter, listen to your heart.

We don't need ceremonies after the death of a pet.
After a death, ceremony helps us express what we could not otherwise express, give honor to the life that was lived, and provide a time and a place for mourners to support one another. We do need ceremonies after the death of pets. (See p. 64.)

29

# When my cat was put to sleep
Mona's story

My Siamese cat, Trixie, was 16. She developed 'catsheimer's' and couldn't remember where things were, like the cat box. I called the vet and made an appointment for the next morning. I prayed that she would die during the night. She did not. I thought I was approaching this logically, and that I would be fine through this process. I bundled her up in a towel and talked to her throughout the drive to the vet. As soon as I walked in, I began to cry. The vet gave me the option of staying with her during the process or just leaving her. I felt it was a disservice to her to abandon her at the end. I opted to stay. He gave her a sedative shot, and I was able to spend a few minutes alone with her before he put her down. I petted her and talked to her throughout, until he pronounced her dead. How did I feel after? I felt tremendous guilt that I "chose" when to end a life. Two months later, the logical side of me is at peace with the decision, but the emotional part of me still feels bad. I'm 46, and I hope I never have to do this again.

manner of your pet's death. This is true whether your pet was killed in an accident, died of an illness, or succumbed to old age. The fact that your pet was euthanized may leave you feeling especially vulnerable and unsettled. You may second-guess yourself or have nagging feelings of guilt. You may find yourself blaming the veterinarian. You may feel drained and numb.

Allow yourself to feel these feelings and think these thoughts. Talk about them with another family member or a friend who understands your love for this pet. Expressing them will render them less powerful and over time, you will grow more sure in your decision to euthanize.

How to mourn

We've said that grief is what you feel on the inside and that mourning is the expression of grief on the outside. Mourning is "grief gone public."

But how do you mourn? Your grief comes naturally to you. It may hurt and you may be surprised at its pain, but it's there, unbidden. But expressing that grief may not come as naturally to you.

After all, in our society we don't "do death." We don't generally talk about it and we're not usually comfortable around people who express their feelings about it. This can be particularly true following the death of a pet. If we tend to minimize the death of a person, think about how we must minimize the death of a pet!

If you try, however, you can find effective ways to mourn and heal. First, think about the people in your life who also loved your pet.

When we put our dog to sleep
Roberta's story

Jackson was a mutt who looked like and had the personality of a Black Lab. My husband Doug and I got him long before we had children. We would lovingly say he was our 'firstborn.'

When Jackson was 13 years and two months old, he was put to sleep. I took Jackson to the hospital by myself; Doug couldn't do it. My first words when his life left him were, "I killed him." I felt that I killed him, although I knew it was his time and this was the way it had to be. I was left alone in the room to be with Jackson and I cried for about 10 or 15 minutes—hard sobs racking my body—and then I was calm. I drove home in a numb state very slowly. When I pulled into the garage, I was surprised that I was home. I couldn't recall the drive home. I walked into the family room; Doug was there. I said, "Jackson's gone." We hugged and cried for a long time. For the first couple of weeks after he died, I thought I heard him or saw him lying around the house.

We had him cremated. We have Jackson's remains in a sealed box, which we keep in the family room along with several pictures of him. We still love him and miss him. He was a great dog.

Talk to them about your thoughts and feelings. They may have thoughts and feelings of their own to share. When it's your turn to listen, listen.

Second, turn to other pet lovers. Other people who understand the joys of pet ownership, who value their pets as much as you do, are often good listeners when you feel the need to talk about your grief. Pet grief support groups, which you may find through your vet's office, are another good resource.

Third, express your grief in other effective ways. Write about it in a journal (or in the middle section of this book!). Cry it out. Paint it out. Sculpt it out. Dance it out. Jog it out. Find an activity that you can pour your grief into and go for it.

It's important that you express your grief. Keeping it inside can cause all kinds of emotional and physical troubles, either now or down the road. And keeping it inside won't help you reconcile your loss. Your journey to healing and to being the best person (and possible future pet owner) you can be requires that you spend the time and the energy now to express your thoughts and feelings.

Yes, mourning is work. But it's good work. It's satisfying work. It's necessary work. So get to work!

Why you don't "get over" your grief

You may have already heard the question, "Are you over it yet?" Or, even worse, be told, "Well, you should be over it by now!" (This is a very common judgment after the death of a pet.) To think that as a human being you "get over" your grief is ludicrous! You don't get over it; you learn to live with it. You learn to integrate it into your life and into the fabric of your being.

You will always, for the rest of our life, feel some grief and sadness over the death of this pet. It will no longer dominate your life, but it will always be there, in the background, reminding you of the love you had for the precious pet that died.

We'll discuss this topic more in Part Three of this book. For now, I'd like for you to think more about the precious life of the animal you loved so much.

WHERE TO TURN FOR HELP

When you are deeply wounded after the death of a pet, you may need more support than your friends and family can provide. In general, our society isn't good at supporting mourners. When pets die, we're typically even worse.

A professional counselor may help you if you feel unable to move forward in your grief. In fact, a good counselor can be something friends and family members can't: an objective listener. A counselor's office can be that safe haven where you can "give voice" to those feelings you're afraid to express elsewhere. What's more, a good counselor will then help you constructively channel those emotions.

There are counselors who specialize in pet loss. There are also support groups for people mourning the death of a beloved pet. In a group, you can connect with others who have experienced similar thoughts and feelings. You will be allowed and encouraged to talk about your grief as much and as often as you like.

The website pet-loss.net maintains a state-by-state guide (also with a link for Canada/International) to pet loss support groups, counselors and pet cemeteries. Click on their "Links & Hotlines" button.

Remember—getting help is a sign of great strength, not a sign of weakness. You deserve to live and love wholly again.

When my mother's dog died
Barbara's story

I helped my elderly mother when her dog Peppy was dying. She kept her on a blanket on the front porch until she breathed her last and then I dug a hole in the back yard and buried her. I remember that the ground was so hard but it felt good to physically put my emotions into the digging.

Mother didn't want another dog for a long time after that. She had had Peppy, her constant friend, for a very long time and mourned her loss. I think, however, that as we get older we can accept death as a part of the life cycle much more readily, having been touched by it many times, and perhaps it is a little easier. Perhaps losing a pet that has loved you unconditionally, always forgiving your bad temper and neglect, who is always glad to see you and asks for only your affection, is more difficult than losing some of your relatives who might not have been such nice people. Perhaps we can see a little bit of the face of God in our loving pets.

Pumpkin the cat
Jesse's story

My cat died when she was almost 19 and I was 18. This cat had been around since I was born. She slept in my bed every night for as long as I can remember. After she died, I had trouble falling asleep. I was more depressed than I have ever been. It was, at the time, the most significant loss I had ever experienced. I didn't go to school or work for a few days. I didn't want to see my friends. I just kind of withdrew for a while. Thinking about her now has brought tears to my eyes. I still miss her, and I don't think I'll ever own another cat.

PART TWO
REMEMBERING

I said that your grief is a journey. But your love for your pet is a journey, too. It began the day that you first met your pet. And it is a journey that never ends.

You see, you will always love your pet. Love doesn't end with death—that is the beauty and power of love. The nature of the relationship changes, yes, but the love does not. You can no longer embrace your pet, but you can always embrace the love you have for her.

Remembering your pet

When a beloved pet dies, she lives on in you through memory. To reconcile your loss, it may help you to actively remember your pet and commemorate the life that was lived. We hope you have someone in your life whom you feel safe to talk with about the pet that died.

It's good to keep talking about your pet. It's good to look at pictures of him. Never let anyone try to take away your memories in a misguided attempt to save you from pain. You need to remember, not forget. Remembering the past makes hoping for the future possible.

Some of the things you can do to keep memories alive are:

- *talk with a friend or family member about favorite memories of times you shared with your pet.*
  Again, others who loved this pet might want to share memories. Or find another pet lover to talk to.

- *make a memory book or memory box.*
  A memory book is a scrapbook dedicated to your pet. In it you can place photos as well as other important small mementos such as ownership papers, sketches, collar tags, etc. If a scrapbook won't hold these items well (because you have too many or they are bulky), place your photos and mementos in a special memory box, instead.

- *keep mementos of the pet that died.*
  You might want to keep a food bowl, a leash, a cage, a special blanket. These are called "linking objects" because they are a physical link to the pet that died. It's normal and natural not only for you to want to keep these objects, but also to want them to be near you when you're missing your pet.

- *look through photo albums at special times,* such as birthdays, holidays, anniversaries or any other times you have a need to bring your memories closer to your heart.

In memory of my special pet

The following section is provided for you to write down special memories of your pet. It is a way for you to mourn (which, you'll remember, means to express your grief outside yourself) and honor your pet's unique and special life. It is also a way for you to capture your memories while they're still fresh in your mind.

Years from now you will be glad you took the time to write about your pet. This section will become a cherished document for you to review whenever you're missing your special companion animal.

In this section I've also included space for you to consider how you can turn your memories into memorials—in other words, how you can help perpetuate the legacy of the pet that died. You can do many things to pay ongoing tribute. You can do many things to continue to demonstrate your love. Be creative and be committed.

If you have a picture of the pet that died, place it here in this book:

What did your pet look like? Write about physical characteristics such as breed, coloring, height, weight, and special markings.

_____

_____

_____

_____

_____

_____

_____

_____

_____

_____

_____

_____

_____

_____

_____

_____

_____

_____

_____

_____

_____

_____

What was your pet's personality? Write about her special behaviors, quirks, facial expressions, and habits.

_____

_____

_____

_____

_____

_____

_____

_____

_____

_____

_____

_____

_____

_____

_____

_____

_____

_____

_____

_____

Write out a funny or meaningful story about your pet.

_____
_____
_____
_____
_____
_____
_____
_____
_____
_____
_____
_____
_____
_____
_____
_____
_____
_____
_____
_____
_____
_____
_____

Make a list of all the things you learned from your pet.

_____

_____

_____

_____

_____

_____

_____

_____

_____

_____

_____

_____

_____

_____

_____

_____

_____

_____

_____

_____

_____

_____

_____

Here you are invited to write about how and why your companion
animal died.

_____

_____

_____

_____

_____

_____

_____

_____

_____

_____

_____

_____

_____

_____

_____

_____

_____

_____

_____

_____

What do you miss the very most about your special pet?

_____

_____

_____

_____

_____

_____

_____

_____

_____

_____

What other things will you always remember about your pet?

_____

_____

_____

_____

_____

_____

_____

_____

_____

_____

In the space below, write a letter to the pet that died. Tell him or her
what is in your head and on your heart.

Dear _____,

_____

_____

_____

Are there any other thoughts and feelings about the death of your pet that you would like to express?

_____

_____

_____

_____

_____

_____

_____

_____

_____

_____

_____

_____

_____

_____

_____

_____

_____

_____

_____

_____

Place another favorite photo of the pet that died (or, if you'd prefer, mementos such as ownership papers, collar tags, etc.) in the space below.

Honey the goat
Luana's story

In 1986 we got two just-weaned goats for our daughter's 4-H project. Butterscotch was a lop-eared Nubian and Honey a Nubian-LaMancha cross. They lived in the back of the garage in a room that opened into a fenced yard. At the same time we had two Toulouse geese. We fed the goats hay and a processed grain mix. The geese got cracked corn.

When the goats were about nine months old, they got into the cracked corn. The corn fermented in their stomachs and poisoned them. The vet hooked them up to IVs in our laundry room. The second day Honey died in my arms. Butterscotch survived. I was very upset, cried a great deal, and blamed myself for Honey's needless death.

Honey was my favorite of the two. She was loving and playful, and much nicer. I felt I had failed her, leaving the corn where they could get to it.

Goats are easy to love and hard to resist. I had never witnessed a death before, had never held anyone while they were dying. I was changed by the experience, saddened and determined to do better by my other pets and those I would have in the future.

PART THREE
HEALING

You loved your pet. And because your love was deep and profound, your grief is deep and profound. This is both normal and necessary. Never be ashamed of your grief over the death of a pet.

It's also normal and necessary for you to express your grief. As I've said, an important distinction to keep in mind is the difference between grief and mourning. Grief is the constellation of thoughts and feelings we have on the inside when a pet dies. Mourning is the outward expression of those thoughts and feelings. If we are to heal, we must not only grieve, we must mourn.

WHAT IS HEALING IN GRIEF?

To heal in grief is to become whole again, to integrate your grief into your self and to learn to continue your changed life with full-ness and meaning. Experiencing a new and changed "wholeness" requires that you not only grieve the death of your companion, but you mourn it, as well.

Healing is a holistic concept that embraces the physical, emotion-al, cognitive, social, and spiritual realms. Note that healing is not the same as curing, which is a medical term that means "remedy-ing" or "correcting." You cannot remedy your grief, but you can reconcile it. You cannot correct your grief, but you can heal it.

All pet owners experience the following six needs after a beloved pet dies. Finding ways to help yourself meet these needs will help you reconcile your grief and move toward healing.

The Six Needs of Mourning

1. Acknowledge the reality of your pet's death.
2. Move toward the pain of the loss.
3. Continue the relationship with the pet that died through memory.
4. Adjust your self-identity.
5. Search for meaning.
6. Continue to receive support from others.

Need 1. Acknowledge the reality of your pet's death.

Whether the death of your pet was sudden or anticipated, acknowledging the full reality of the loss may take weeks or months. You may come home still expecting your pet to greet you at the door. You may wake up still expecting your pet to be there, as always, at your bedside. You may reach down to stroke your pet only to find he is no longer there. Getting used to the idea that your pet is gone will take some time. You may move back and forth between protesting and embracing the reality of the death. You may also find that while your head fully understands the death, your heart needs more time and compassion in acknowledging the reality.

Need 2. Move toward the pain of the loss.

Experiencing your thoughts and feelings about the death of your pet, with all of their intensity, is a difficult but important need. You may find that you are trying to distract yourself from your pain by keeping busy or avoiding the places that most remind you of your pet. While you cannot–and should not try to–confront all of your pain at once, neither should you try to avoid it. "Dose" yourself with your painful feelings of grief. Let them in, a little bit at a time. Allow yourself to cry. Be sad when you feel the need to be sad.

Need 3. Continue the relationship with the pet that died through memory.

Do we still have a relationship with a pet that has died? Our memories allow our pets to live on in us. We can revisit those memories whenever we want, simply by opening our hearts and turning our mind's eye to the past. Embracing your memories–both happy and sad–can be a very slow and, at times, painful process that occurs in small steps. But remembering the past makes hoping for the future possible.

Need 4. Adjust your self-identity.

Part of your self-identity comes from being a pet owner. You probably think of yourself as your pet's caretaker. You may also consider your pet a big part of what makes your life complete. Others may also think of you in relation to your pet. You may be the guy who always walked the big black dog around the neighborhood or the friend whose cat always jumped on laps. Now that your pet has died, the way you define yourself and the way others define you has changed. Adjusting to this change is a central need of mourning.

Need 5. Search for meaning.

When a pet dies, we naturally question the meaning and purpose of pets in our lives. Coming to terms with these questions is another need we must meet if we are to progress in our grief journeys. Why did God give us pets? Why do many of them only live such a brief time? What happens to pets after they die? Will I ever be ready to love another pet? Move at your own pace as you allow yourself to think and feel through these kinds of questions and know that it is the asking, not the finding of concrete answers, that is important.

Need 6. Continue to receive support from others.

You will never stop needing the love and support of others because you never "get over" your grief. As you learn to reconcile your grief over the death of your pet, you will need help less intensely and less often, but you will always need your friends and family members to listen and support you in your continuing grief journey. Talking to other pet owners who have experienced the death of a pet can be one important way to meet this need.

To meet these six needs, you must actively mourn the death of your special pet. You must find ways—ways that really work for you—to express your grief outside yourself. Mourning is indeed work, and it is work that requires your time and effort. Yes, you are wounded, but with commitment and intention you can and will become whole again.

You see, I believe that you must "set your intention" to heal. Intention is defined as being conscious of what you want to experience. A close cousin to "affirmation," it is using the power of positive thought to produce a desired result.

When you set your intention to heal in grief, you make a true commitment to positively influence the course of your journey. You choose between being what I call a "passive witness" or an "active participant" in your grief. You tell yourself that you can and will reach out for support in your grief, and that you will learn to live and love wholly again.

I'm sure you have heard the tired cliché: Time heals all wounds. Yet, time alone has little to do with healing. To heal, you must be willing to learn about the mystery of the grief journey. It can't be fixed or "resolved;" it can only be soothed and reconciled through actively expressing your many thoughts and feelings.

When our dog died
Annette's story

My pet was a Golden Retriever named Juno and she was 10 when she died. She had brain cancer for a year before she died, and was being treated with Prednisone, which affected her liver and heart. She weakened over that year, and on the day of her death, she was breathing hard and fast. She was in heart failure. She died in my husband's arms. She was very special to us because we bought her as a puppy when we had been married only a year. She was our constant companion.

The day of her death, I cried and hugged her. I cried just as much for my husband as for myself because he was very close to her and he was crying and holding her, and I knew he was devastated. For several weeks after her death, I couldn't tell anyone about her dying without getting choked up. I felt sad for her and the pain she had endured. I also felt fortunate that she died naturally and that we didn't have to put her down, because we had been considering it.

Juno died on Labor Day while we were visiting my husband's parents in Wyoming. We put her in a large Rubbermaid container and taped it shut. We buried her in an Aspen grove in their yard where they had buried their dog. For a burial ceremony, my father-in-law led us in prayer.

Today, almost three years later, I remember her as "The Best Dog." We could always tell what she was thinking because of her facial expressions. She loved to be with us and she would "talk" to us with snorting noises. We now have a 1½ year old Golden, and I miss the fact that Juno was so obedient (I've forgotten her puppy years!). I cry again when I think of how good she was and how much she must have suffered while she was sick.

HOW OTHERS CAN HELP YOU:
THREE ESSENTIALS

While there are a number of ways that people who care about you might reach out to help you after the death of a special pet, here are three important and fundamental helping goals. Effective helpers will help you:

1. *Have "companions" in your journey.*
These people serve as companions though whom your suffering can be affirmed. They know that real compassion comes out of "walking with" you, not ahead of you or behind you. The word grieve means "to bear a heavy burden." Those who companion you in your grief realize that as they help bear your burden of sorrow, they give you hope that something good will come of it.

2. *Encounter the presence of your loss.*
These are the people who understand the need for you to revisit and recount the pain of your loss. They listen to you as you "tell your story" and provide a safe place for you to openly mourn. They do not downplay the loss because it was the loss of a pet; instead, they seem to understand that this death has profoundly affected you and that you need to talk about it. Essentially, they give you an invitation to take the grief that is inside you and share it outside yourself.

3. *Embrace hope.*
These are the people who help you sustain the presence of hope even as you feel separated from those things that make life worth living. They can be present to you in your loss, yet bring you a sense of trust in yourself that you can and will heal.

Reconciling your grief

You may have heard that your grief journey's end will come when you resolve, or recover from, your grief. But your journey will never end. Soften, yes, but end, no. People do not "get over" the death of a pet.

Reconciliation is a term I find more appropriate for what occurs as you work to move forward in life without the physical presence of your pet. With reconciliation comes a renewed sense of energy and confidence, an ability to fully acknowledge the reality of the death and a capacity to become re-involved in the activities of living.

In reconciliation, the sharp, ever-present pain of grief gives rise to a renewed sense of meaning and purpose. Your feelings of loss over the death of your pet will not completely disappear, yet they will soften, and the intense pangs of grief will become less frequent. While you realize that your pet will never be forgotten, you will know that your life can and will move forward and be filled with hope and joy once again.

Be patient and tolerant with yourself as you work to meet your six central needs of mourning after your pet dies. Work to express your grief and set your intention to heal. Trust in your journey to reconciliation.

Nurturing yourself in five important realms

Grief affects every part of our being. When we are grieving, we must learn to nurture ourselves in all five aspects of our lives: physically; emotionally; cognitively; socially; and spiritually. Following are a few suggestions to help you help yourself heal by focusing on each of the five areas.

The physical realm

As we have said, your body may be letting you know it feels distressed. You can help your body cope with the stress of your grief by taking good care of it. Stop smoking, eat healthfully, exercise, and get adequate rest. Get a physical exam and ask your doctor what you should be doing to improve your health. Remember that taking poor care of your body right now will only complicate your grief journey.

The emotional realm

Earlier in this book we explored some of the emotions that are often part of the grief experience after the death of a special companion animal. These emotions reflect that you have special needs that require support from both outside yourself and inside yourself. The important thing to remember is that we honor our emotions when we pay attention to them and find ways to express them.

The cognitive realm

Your mind is the intellectual ability to think, absorb information, make decisions, and reason logically. Without doubt, you have special needs in the cognitive realm of your grief experience. Just as your body and emotions let you know you have experienced being "torn apart," your mind has also, in effect, been torn apart. Don't be surprised if you struggle with short-term memory problems, have trouble making simple decisions, and think you may be going crazy. Essentially, your mind is in a state of disorientation and confusion.

Early in your grief, you may find it helpful to allow yourself to "suspend" all thought and purposefulness for a time. Allow yourself to just "be." Later in your journey after the death of a pet, remember that your cognitive powers are quite remarkable. Willing yourself to think something can in fact help make that something come to be. Think about your desired reality to heal in grief and make it happen.

The social realm

You may have noticed that since the death of your pet you feel a disconnection from the world around you. You are grieving the loss of a very personal relationship—one that most people outside your household can't comprehend. This can cause you to feel separate or distanced from everyone else. But you must remember that reaching out to friends and family is essential to your healing. When you reach out to others, you are beginning to reconnect. Your link to family, friends, and community is vital to your sense of well-being and belonging. If you don't nurture the warm, loving relationships in your life, you will probably continue to feel disconnected and isolated. You may even withdraw into your own small world and grieve, but not mourn. Isolation can then become the barrier that keeps your grief from softening over time.

The spiritual realm

When your pet dies, your spirit is wounded. You may also have many spiritual questions to which there are no easy answers. Why did my pet have to die? Why now? Why this way? What happens to pets after they die? Wrestling with these questions and feeling the pain of the loss deep in your soul can zap your energy and fill you with doubt. Take care of your spiritual self by meditating, praying, and spending time in quiet contemplation. If you have doubt about your capacity to connect with God and the world around you, try to approach the world with the openness of a child. Embrace the pleasure that comes from the simple sights, smells, and sounds that greet your senses. You can and will find yourself rediscovering the essentials within your soul and the spirit of the world around you.

The power of ritual
Paul's story

When I was young, our dog, a white-and-tan, good-natured beagle named Snoopy, died from cancer. His death haunted all of us in the family. I kept seeing him running around the house, ears like sailplanes, tongue seeking the nearest face, complacent in his unending devotion to us. But his death had been unpleasant to see, and costly at a time when our family could afford neither the emotional trauma nor the expense. The younger ones in the family—my brother, especially—had trouble grappling with how unnecessary, how unfair it was to have had such a small, vibrant life taken from us that way. The cost of trying to keep our dog alive made us uneasy, too, in ways we couldn't quite fathom. In the grown-up world, it seemed at the time, there were strange things that tainted noble struggles, elements that had nothing to do with an animal's devotion. I felt my parents had been relieved to be rid of the burden at last, although they never said as much, and comforted us as best they could.

But after we gave Snoopy a burial in the back yard, in a deep grave where the wooded hill still meets the open field, my younger brother began trooping the few hundred yards to the gravesite—marked with a crude wooden cross and Snoopy's collar—and playing Taps in the evenings. At first I treated the ritual with detached scorn; then, as he kept it up over the course of several weeks, I began to ridicule him, to vent my anger for having to watch him act like a baby. Was he going to keep blowing that silly horn for the rest of his life? And how dare he think the dog was more valuable to him than anybody else. How dare he make such a show of his sorrow.

We had more animals after Snoopy, some who were just as devoted to us and who lived long, happy lives. Our family rarely mentioned Snoopy over the years, until my father just recently conjured up the memory of my brother and his horn. Some 35 years after the last note echoed over Snoopy's grave, my father remembered standing by the living room window, looking out while my brother played Taps, and being affected by it almost to the point of tears. "That really got me," my father said, and I suddenly filled with a dizzying array of emotions—despair, because I had reacted in a completely opposite way to my father; anger, because I was the one, it turned out, who had been acting like the baby; wonder, because my father had held such a vivid image for so many years; melancholy, for all the lost moments in the life of our family that we may never share together, not even as memories.

But I also felt proud of my brother, because he had played his horn long after I'd started harassing him, proud because he did what he felt necessary, and how he persevered, as he does to this day, in acting from his heart and not for show. He buried our dog with full honors, and now, listening to my father, who is nearing the end of his own life, I couldn't stop the tears from welling, thinking about how my brother, in sending notes across the warm summer evening, had touched the heart of my father and the core of what it really means to be human.

Celebrating your pet's life

As we have acknowledged repeatedly in this book, your pet was part of your family. Your pet was a love of your life.

When a person dies, we hold a ceremony. Funerals help us acknowledge the reality of the death, remember the person who died, honor the life that was lived, and provide support to mourners. They also give us a forum for saying goodbye.

Pets deserve funerals, too. But more important, as I always say, funerals are for the living. For your sake and for your family's sake, I hope you had a ceremony at the time of your pet's death. Ceremonies help us express what we are incapable of expressing in mere words. I'm sure you found it healing and gratifying.

Ceremony ideas

If you didn't have a ceremony at the time of death, it's not too late! You can still have a very meaningful ceremony, perhaps on your pet's birthday or anniversary of the death. It doesn't have to be complicated or time-consuming. Just a few special words and the opening of your heart are all that is required. Here are a few ideas:

- Gather together the people who loved your pet or who simply love you. Meet in a place where your pet spent happy times. Ask each person to share a special memory or something they miss about her. End with a prayer.

- If your pet was cremated, have a scattering ceremony. Scatter your pet's cremated remains somewhere meaningful to you and your pet. (Or you may choose to bury the remains.) As you scatter them, say out loud the lessons you learned from your pet.

• Hold a candle-lighting ceremony. Put a large pillar candle in the center of a table and gather around the table. Light the center candle. Give each person a votive candle and ask each person to share a memory about the pet. As each person speaks, he should light his candle. Tell everyone that the lit candles represent the love they have that will always be alight inside them for the special pet that died. (Every Monday night a website called petloss.com sponsors a web-based candle-lighting ceremony. You might want to participate.)

What other ceremony ideas can you think of? Do something special in honor of your beloved companion animal. He or she was worth it, right?

A ceremony for our dog
Mark's story

I have had dogs all of my life and the loss of one three years ago was particularly tough. We had had Bambi for eight years. We got her when my boys were two and four, so they were very close to her and she was great with them. She was a mutt from my in-laws' farm but was a world champion in the eyes of our family and those who knew her.

After she was killed by a car near our house, I asked the kids what they wanted to do. Immediately they told me they wanted to bury her in a special place. They decided that the big pine tree back by the "park" on our property would be best. I went back and dug the grave. We all went back and said some nice things about her, shared a prayer and buried her. Both boys picked out pictures of her they liked that had been taken through the years and have them framed and in their rooms. Her grave is marked and she will always be fondly remembered by my family.

Many years ago I heard it said that the cruelest thing God did was make us outlive our dogs. I have to agree at times.

Memorializing your pet

In addition to holding a ceremony, you might also like to memorialize your pet in an ongoing way. Some of these ideas provide you with a "place" to remember and mourn your pet.

Following are just a handful of ideas; I'm sure you have many creative ideas of your own. Choose something that holds meaning for you and the pet that died.

• Plant a garden in memory of your pet. Choose plants that remind you of her or are meaningful to you in some way. Cats love catmint and dogwood is an obvious choice for a dog. Lovely bleeding heart can be a perennial reminder of your love for any animal.

• Help children learn to become responsible pet owners. If you own horses, invite children's groups to visit your horses and learn about how to take care of them. You might even give each child a short ride.

• Get involved in organizations that support therapeutic uses for pets. Equine therapy helps many injured and developmentally disabled people. Visiting dogs bring joy to elderly people in nursing homes.

• Donate a bench in a park where your dog liked to play.

• Give money to your local animal shelter in your pet's name.

• Donate to an organization that supports the type of animal you loved. For example, the American Federation of Aviculture educates the public about keeping and breeding birds in captivity. If you are a bird lover, your membership in this association helps foster responsible bird-human relationships across the United States.

- Buy a special piece of artwork and place it in your home. For a permanent, in-home reminder of your pet, you may want to seek out or commission a sculpture or a painting that depicts a pet like yours. Some painters can paint your pet from a good photo.

- Wear something that physically denotes your loss. As I mentioned earlier, the ancient Egyptians shaved off their eyebrows when their cats died. The Victorians wore black armbands after a death. Perhaps you could create a photo button or locket to wear to express your grief.

Remember that memorializing your pet doesn't have to be expensive or lavish. A simple homemade grave marker or a special photo that you've enlarged, framed and hung in your family room might suffice. But do memorialize. You'll feel good about honoring the life of your special pet and keeping his memory alive.

The website lastingfriends.com sells a number of products specifically designed to help you memorialize your pet. These include garden steppingstones, personalized picture frames, cremation urns and much more.

When it's time to consider getting another pet

Will you ever feel ready to parent a new pet? The answer is maybe.

Widows ask me sometimes when they should remarry. Bereaved parents sometimes ask me when or if they should have another child. I tell them that they should wait until they are ready to love wholly again. Of course they will always mourn the loss of the person who died. Of course they will always miss this unique person, who could never, ever, be replaced. But there are other people to love in this world and when they feel ready to give and receive love again, they should.

So it should be after the death of a pet.

Will you love the new pet as much? This question can only be answered in hindsight. You may end up loving your new pet equally but differently. You may love your new pet less, yet still love him. Your new pet may even end up being the animal "love of your life." What is the worst case scenario? That you would not love the pet at all and would give her up for adoption? That rarely happens with pet lovers.

Ultimately, the decision to get a new pet is personal and highly individual and shouldn't be rushed into. But your openness to accepting the joys of a new animal relationship will be affected by how intentionally you mourned the death of your special pet.

I always encourage people to mourn well so they can go on to live and love well again. If you do not actively and intentionally express your grief outside of yourself, if you do not examine your thoughts and feelings and give them play, you may not arrive at a place in which you can truly open your heart to the love and companionship of a new animal.

In grief, you are transformed. You are forever changed. Yet if you do the work of mourning and allow yourself to be vulnerable again, you can open yourself to the joys of new and delightful animal companions.

THE ADOPTION OPTION

Every year, 8-12 million unwanted companion animals are given to shelters. If and when you're ready to think about getting another pet, visit your local animal shelter first. Don't fall victim to the myth that shelter animals are problem animals. Many, many of these millions of animals are healthy and loving and well-behaved—they just had problem owners!

The American Society for the Prevention of Cruelty to Animals (ASPCA) says their goal is to make pet adoption the first option for all Americans. Visit aspca.petfinder.org to search a network of more than 2,000 shelters. You'll feel good that you're saving a life and in return, getting a lifetime of love and companionship.

If and when you feel ready to seriously consider getting a new companion animal, it's OK to get your feet wet little by little. Visit your local animal shelter several times. Stop by a reputable pet store. Call a breeder or two and ask if you can come by just to look. When you're in the company of the new animals, note how you feel. Do you feel predominantly hopeful and happy? Or do you feel mostly sad and mournful? If you fall into the latter camp, you may need more time and attention to your mourning before you're ready to get a new pet.

And sometimes a new pet will find you. A friend may call needing homes for a litter of new kittens. Or a neighbor may mention a puppy she saw at the animal shelter. Or you might be offered a bird to adopt or a foal to raise.

I believe in looking for signs in life. Look for signs that you are ready to accept a new pet. You might even look for signs from your beloved pet that died telling you you're ready. If a new pet finds you, maybe that's a sign. Maybe you're ready to live and love again.

Scrumpy Junior
Jeanette's story

In June of 1999, our nine-year-old daughter Jeanette, affectionately known in our house as Scrumpy, picked out a guinea pig at the local pet store. The store owner said this pig would be the most difficult to bond with because it was already six months old, and that maybe she should choose a younger one. But Jeanette's mind was set; she chose and paid for with her own money the underdog brown pig with white markings and named her Scrumpy Junior.

Jeanette understood that she needed to play with Scrumy Junior for at least one hour a day, and take care of the cage every day as well. And through the four years, Jeanette kept to that promise. It was a common sight to see Jeanette walking around the house with her pig, or sitting in front of the TV petting her pig and talking to her. She always spoke so sweetly to Scrumpy Jr. And the pig would purr back at Jeanette, a sign that the pig had bonded.

On June 1, 2003, Jeanette, who was now 13, screamed down the stairs to come quick, something was wrong. When I picked up Scrumpy Jr., the pig had no lower body tone. Jeanette started to cry and plead for me to do something. The pig was obviously distressed and trying to find somewhere to hide, but was unable to move well.

We arrived at the vet hospital, with Scrumpy Jr. whining now like a puppy, and the doctor swept Scrumpy Jr. away and came out a few minutes later looking for Jeanette. The doctor spoke right at her and asked if she wanted to see Scrumpy Jr. while they discussed what was happening. Poor little Scrumpy Jr. was hooked up with electrodes and looked tiny on the large table. She was now unconscious. Jeanette asked if it was something she did, and the Vet assured her that no, the pig wasn't poisoned or harmed, it was just her time. Scrumpy Jr. was four, a common age for guinea pigs to die of old age. The doctor said she looked healthy, with a shiny coat and eyes; she had obviously been well taken care of.

(cont.)

The vet told Jeanette that she didn't think Scrumpy would make it, and asked if Jeanette wanted her euthanized. Without hesitation, but through horrific sobs, Jeanette said yes, that to keep her around would only be for Jeanette, and not what was right for Scrumpy Jr.

The doctor asked if Jeanette wanted to stay while they put the needle in Scrumpy. Jeanette stayed, and petted and kissed and talked with Scrumpy Jr., telling her how much she loved her and would miss her, and that she was the best pig ever, until the vet said that she was gone. With our whole family standing there, we said our last goodbyes.

Back at home, Jeanette put her pig in a box with some of her favorite toys, a shirt that smelled like Jeanette, and her picture. We buried her in a very deep hole in the backyard, had a brief ceremony, and marked the grave with a marble marker with her name and the dates of her life on it. Jeanette still thinks of her pig frequently and speaks of her every time we pass the vet hospital. Scrumpy Jr. was a wonderful addition to Jeanette's life and helped her to understand that love and loss are intertwined.

A FINAL WORD

"Lord, help me to be the person my dog thinks I am."
Anonymous

It was Anatole France who poignantly observed, "Until one has loved an animal, a part of one's soul remains unawakened." Like me, you made a choice to awaken your soul by giving love to and receiving love from your precious pet. And, like me, you have come to know the pain of your grief.

Sorrow is an inescapable dimension of our capacity to deeply bond with our pets. We suffer in our loss because we have loved. And in our suffering, we realize our animal friends have often been great teachers about life, particularly regarding the vital importance of unconditional love. I don't fully understand how (and I don't think I have to), but my pets have always helped me realize how precious life really is—and just how connected we all are to each other and to God. My pets have helped me stay in the moment rather than concern myself with yesterday or tomorrow.

While it hurts to suffer the loss of our pets, I believe the alternative is apathy and aloneness. Apathy literally means the inability to suffer, and it results in a lifestyle that avoids connected relationships to preclude suffering. I suspect you have met people who have said to you things like, "I could never have pets...I would get too close to them and then they would die." These people choose not to love a pet so they can avoid the pain of grief. What they don't realize that you and I do is that they also choose to miss out on an indescribable kindred connection.

It was Kahlil Gibran who wrote, "When you are sorrowful, look again in your heart, and you shall see that in truth you are weeping for that which has been your delight." As I remember my beloved pets, I can honestly say they have been my delights. How about you?

As I close out this book, I'm sitting here in the foothills of Colorado remembering my Siberian Husky Tasha. My wife Sue and I got her during our second year of marriage. We often referred to her as our first and furriest child. She brought 13 years of happiness to our family. As three children entered her life, she welcomed them with open paws.

Siberians love children and that was apparent from the moment we brought each child home. When Megan, Chris, and Jaimie came home for the first time, she had this lovely ritual of putting her nose against each baby's nose as if to say, "Welcome to the Wolfelt family. Even though I preceded you here I'm glad to meet you. I will protect and care for you as you grow from infancy to toddlerhood to childhood. We will share in this family together. I will love you always and forever."

If Tasha could have talked, that is exactly what she would have said.

As Tasha aged, she developed arthritis and grew less active. Yet, her love was always present in our lives. Without doubt, she was an integral part of the family. She was also an integral part of my work life.

My house is next door to my company, which is called The Center for Loss. She often walked over to the Center to visit my clients and workshop participants.

One day Tasha snuggled up next to a workshop participant–an older man who was enjoying the views from the deck–and nudged him in such a way that he had to put his arm around her. The man's wife of more than 50 years had recently died. Upon his return home to California, he wrote me a letter and said that while I was helpful and supportive to him in his mourning, his most sacred moment had been when Tasha invited his touch. It was as if Tasha knew in her soul that this man was hurting and she reached out to minister to him. This moment became the turning point for this man–the moment at which he made the conscious choice to actively mourn his wife and go on to discover renewal in his life.

In her 13th year, Tasha slowed down even more, her arthritis getting the best of her. She took her medication gladly and tried to keep going for our family as much if not more than for herself.

And then one summer afternoon she simply walked off the end of the foothill we live on as if to say, "I know my life is over and I want to spare you the pain of my loss." A passing jogger saw her in the brush and was kind enough to seek us out and tell us. When I came to Tasha she just looked up at me with her beautiful clear blue eyes in a way that said, "My journey has come to an end. I have loved being a part of this family. Thank you, but let me go."

I cried openly as I carried her and placed her in the back of my car. Our family of five all accompanied her to the veterinarian's office. We held her, we petted her, we talked to her, we loved her one last time and then she closed her eyes and died.

For 13 wonderful years she had been a special member of our family. It didn't feel the same without her. Yes, "a faithful friend is the medicine of life"—Ecclesiastes 6:26.

You, too, have lost a faithful friend and my sincere hope is that this little book is a small, quiet voice of support for you. Right now, take a moment to close your eyes, open your heart, and remember how it felt to touch and be touched by your precious pet.

Bless you. I hope we meet one day.

THE PET LOVER'S CODE
TEN INALIENABLE RIGHTS AFTER THE DEATH
OF A SPECIAL COMPANION ANIMAL

Though you should reach out to others as you journey through grief,
you should not feel obligated to accept the unhelpful responses you
may receive from some people. You are the one who is grieving, and
as such, you have certain "rights" no one should try to take away
from you.

The following list is intended both to empower you to heal and to
decide how others can and cannot help. This is not to discourage
you from reaching out to others for help, but rather to assist you in
distinguishing useful responses from hurtful ones.

1. You have the right to grieve the death of a pet.
    You loved your pet. Your pet loved you. You had a strong and pro-
    found relationship. You have every right to grieve this death. You
    need to grieve this death. You also need to mourn this death
    (express your grief outside yourself).

2. You have the right to talk about your grief.
    Talking about your grief will help you heal. Seek out others who
    will allow you to talk about your grief. Other pet lovers who have
    experienced the death of a pet often make good listeners at this
    time. If at times you don't feel like talking, you also have the right
    to be silent.

3. You have the right to feel a variety of emotions.
    Confusion, anger, guilt, and relief are just a few of the emotions
    you might feel as part of your grief journey after the death of a pet.
    Feelings aren't right or wrong; they just are.

4. You have the right to be tolerant of your physical and emotional limits. After the death of a pet, your feelings of loss and sadness will probably leave you feeling fatigued. Respect what your body and mind are telling you. Get daily rest. Eat balanced meals. And don't allow others to push you into doing things you don't feel like doing.

5. You have the right to experience "griefbursts." Sometimes, out of nowhere, a powerful surge of grief may overcome you. This can be frightening, but it is normal and natural.

6. You have the right to make use of ritual. After a pet dies, you can harness the power of ritual to help you heal. Plan a ceremony that includes everyone who loved your pet.

7. You have the right to embrace your spirituality. At times of loss, it is natural to turn to your faith or spirituality. Engaging your spirituality by attending church or other place of worship, praying, or spending time alone in nature may help you better understand and reconcile your loss.

8. You have the right to search for meaning. You may find yourself asking, "Why did my pet die? Why this way? Why now?" Some of your questions may have answers, but some may not. Ask them anyway.

9. You have the right to treasure your memories. Memories are one of the best legacies that exist after the death of a special companion animal. Instead of ignoring your memories, find ways to capture them and treasure them always.

10. You have the right to move toward your grief and heal. Reconciling your grief after the death of a pet may not happen quickly. Remember, grief is best experienced in "doses." Be patient and tolerant with yourself and avoid people who are impatient and intolerant with you. Neither you nor those around you must forget that the death of a beloved pet changes your life forever.

RESOURCES

Following are some additional resources you might find helpful
in your journey through grief after the death of a special companion
animal.

Books:

Goodbye, Friend, Gary Kowalski, Stillpoint Publishing, 1997.

Grieving the Death of a Pet, Betty J. Carneck, Augsburg Books, 2003.

Kindred Spirits, Allen M. Schoen, D.V.M., Broadway Books, 2001.

The Loss of a Pet, Wallace Sife, Ph.D., Howell Book House, 1998

Websites:

www.alln.org
(Animal Love and Loss network)

www.centerforloss.com
(This is the website of my organization, the Center for Loss.)

www.in-memory-of-pets.com

www.lastingfriends.com

www.petloss.com

www.pet-loss.net
(This site maintains an excellent listing of pet loss support groups, counselors,
and pet cemeteries as well as pet loss hotlines and other websites with helpful
pet loss information.)

ALSO BY ALAN WOLFELT

UNDERSTANDING YOUR GRIEF
TEN ESSENTIAL TOUCHSTONES FOR
FINDING HOPE AND HEALING YOUR HEART

One of North America's leading grief educators, Dr. Alan
Wolfelt has written many books about healing in grief.
This new book is his most comprehensive, covering the
essential lessons that mourners have taught him in his
three decades of working with the bereaved.

In compassionate, down-to-earth language, *Understanding Your Grief*
describes ten touchstones—or trail markers—that are essential physical,
emotional, cognitive, social, and spiritual signs for mourners to look for
on their journey through grief.

The Ten Essential Touchstones:

1. Open to the presence of your loss.
2. Dispel misconceptions about grief.
3. Embrace the uniqueness of your grief.
4. Explore your feelings of loss.
5. Recognize you are not crazy.
6. Understand the six needs of mourning.
7. Nurture yourself.
8. Reach out for help.
9. Seek reconciliation, not resolution.
10. Appreciate your transformation.

The companion journal is an ideal place to write down your thoughts
and feelings as you explore the ten essential touchstones.

ISBN 978-1-879651-35-7 • 176 pages • softcover • $14.95
(plus shipping and handling)

ALSO BY ALAN WOLFELT

THE JOURNEY THROUGH GRIEF
REFLECTIONS ON HEALING
SECOND EDITION

This popular hardcover book makes a wonderful gift for those who grieve, helping them gently engage in the work of mourning. Comforting and nurturing, *The Journey Through Grief* doses mourners with the six needs of mourning, helping them soothe themselves at the same time it helps them heal.

Back by popular demand, we are now offering *The Journey Through Grief* again in hardcover. The hardcover version of this beautiful book makes a wonderful, healing gift for the newly bereaved.

This revised, second edition of *The Journey Through Grief* takes Dr. Wolfelt's popular book of reflections and adds space for guided journaling, asking readers thoughtful questions about their unique mourning needs and providing room to write responses.

The Journey Through Grief is organized around the six needs that all mourners must yield to—indeed embrace—if they are to go on to find continued meaning in life and living. Following a short explanation of each mourning need is a series of brief, spiritual passages that, when read slowly and reflectively, help mourners work through their unique thoughts and feelings. *The Journey Through Grief* is being used by many faith communities as part of their grief support programs.

ISBN 978-1-879651-11-1 • hardcover • 176 pages • $21.95
(plus additional shipping and handling)

ALSO BY ALAN WOLFELT

HEALING YOUR GRIEVING HEART
100 PRACTICAL IDEAS

When someone loved dies, we must express our grief if we are to heal. In other words, we must mourn. But knowing how to mourn doesn't always come naturally.

This book offers 100 practical ideas to help you practice self-compassion. Some of the ideas teach you the principles of grief and mourning. The remainder offer practical, action-oriented tips for embracing your grief. Each also suggests a carpe diem, which will help you seize the day by helping you move toward healing today.

ISBN 978-1-879651-25-8 • 128 pages • softcover • $11.95
(plus additional shipping and handling)

ALSO BY ALAN WOLFELT

HEALING YOUR GRIEVING HEART FOR KIDS
100 PRACTICAL IDEAS

Simple advice and activities for children after a death. An idea book for young and middle readers (6-12 year-olds) grieving the death of someone loved. The text is simple and straight-forward, teaching children about grief and affirming that their thoughts and feelings are not only normal but necessary. Page after page of age-appropriate activities and gentle, healing guidance.

ISBN 978-1-879651-27-2 • 128 pages • Softcover • $11.95
(plus additional shipping and handling)